The Manda

Helen Budge

The Mandarin Tree

Acknowledgements

I would like to thank all those who have contributed to this book.

I am particularly indebted to prize-winning poet Kevin Gillam, who edited and provided the foreword for this collection.

I would also like to thank the six critical readers who provided me with invaluable feedback. They are Marie Finlay, Athena Georgiou, Jenny Hetherington, Gae Oaten, Jan Rodgers and Trish Versteegen.

And thank you to editor and writer Michèle Drouart, who has always supported my writing, in its various genres, through her encyclopedic and expert knowledge of the English language and its idiosyncrasies.

I am also grateful to all the women at Eden Corner, who triggered many of the bird poems. You know who you are!

Thank you, too, to those friends and family who have listened to and read some of the poems. It helps to have an appreciative audience. A special mention to writer and friend the late Robert Jeffreys, whose constant encouragement and belief in my work made me keep writing.

Last but not least, a huge thank you to Stephen Matthews at Ginninderra Press for his offer to publish *The Mandarin Tree*.

The Mandarin Tree
ISBN 978 1 76109 379 1
Copyright © text Helen Budge 2022
Cover design: Andrew Budge

First published 2022 by
GINNINDERRA PRESS
PO Box 3461 Port Adelaide 5015
www.ginninderrapress.com.au

Contents

Foreword

Welcome to the wonders of *The Mandarin Tree*. Here is a body of poetry that truly achieves the nuance and spirit of the craft; poetry that focuses, enhances and reflects upon moments in nature, thought and life.

There are poems imbued with stunning imagery, such as the opening lines from 'Magpie': 'What a singer it is / warbling its welcome to the day / with full-throated panache, / calling up other mornings, / other places.'

Others contain carefully crafted rhythm – these lines from 'Nocturne': 'How clean, how clear, / how tumultuous, / how measured / the flow of / love, of pain.'

Some poems poke and prod, leaving us to ponder, such as in 'Rationality': 'Where does the wildness go? / I want to know. / Does it sink deep / too deep to surface? / Can't wild thoughts / be public?'

Closure too is deftly handled, such as in 'A Winter View': 'Death has no particular season, / Winter has a life of its own.'

The diction choices throughout are sharp and illuminating, and the attention to form gives each poem vitality, willing us to embrace the moment.

I invite you to rest beneath the dappled canopy and taste the fruit of *The Mandarin Tree*.

Kevin Gillam

Spaces

Air

The day is hot and still.
Smoke and jasmine,
scent the air.
A magpie sings,
waves lap the shore.
Four boys,
shouting and laughing,
anchor their boat.
I savour this moment
on a scorched earth
swept by plague.

Day Breaks

Tender, tinged pink,
delicate, vulnerable,
a rose
beginning to bloom.
Darkness hides
the thorns,
the open wound.

Sleepless

It is night.
The tide is high.
I cannot sleep.
Through the open window
An owl's haunting call
floats over the incessant beat
of waves hitting the shore.

With morning
the constant hum of cars
intrudes.
The owl is silent.
A dove is cooing.

Day Is Beginning

Welcome to the waking world,
black night is lightening,
the grass is drenched with dew.
Come, open your eyes,
see the softness of the morning,
listen to the soundless stirring,
feel the air breathing,
yes, come, open your eyes,
day is beginning.

Awakening

So this is what waking is,
this slow, growing sweetness,
this peacefulness
and the sound of the sea,
your breathing,
the soft morning light
tinged pink
and your body,
warm, still sleeping.

This is just to tell you...

I saw
a dove's egg
on the brick path
this morning.

A fragile oval
of perfection
out of place
under the grapevine

Last night's
wild wind
threw it there.
I thought of you.

Path

Salty air lifts the spirits
on this cliff path
above the sea.
The soothing swish of waves
calms the roar of speeding engines.

I am between two worlds:
the vast sea from which we came;
the manufactured world of frantic beings
forgetful of the moment they are in.

Highway

On a clear blue morning
three black swans flying north
bring childhood dreams,
magical stories, a
river of glass
infinitely broad and shining,
ancient godlike trees
sprouting leafy crowns.
And here I am
in a traffic jam
on a bitumen road.

Cirrus

A solitary cirrus
floating in the sky,
why? Oh heavens, why?'

Rationality

Thoughts crash the consciousness
wave after wave,
surf in, frothing
and tumbling, are
sucked back
and return
suitable for distribution
and consumption.

Where does the wildness go?
I want to know.
Does it sink deep
too deep to surface?
Can't wild thoughts
be public?

What is there to fear?
Thoughts are insubstantial,
mere tremblings of the mind.
they are not guns,
nor unexploded bombs.
But only seem so.

Sorrow

Just when you think
you've beaten sorrow
up it creeps
from a kind word
like a small wave
hidden by the dumper
you can see
rising, swelling, curling
from a flat blue sea.
You dive
into the dumper
and emerge unscathed.
But its smaller backup
grabs you,
tumbles and flays you
into the deep.

Sorrow is a sneak.
Kindness is its ally.

A Singing Place

A singing place
of pine trees and sea
is sullied.
A pernicious weed,
an insidious, creeping fear
spread its demon roots there.
A rampant nightmare
grew and grew.
Light was lost,
life choked.

Nocturne

This morning
I listened to
Chopin's Nocturnes
and this evening too.
How sad,
how beautiful
these conversations
between the piano
and the self.
How clean,
how clear,
how tumultuous,
how measured
the flow of
love, of pain.

A Cold Wind

A cold wind of discontent
whips and penetrates
protected spaces.
It numbs and freezes action
to destructive silence.
An exposed child cries
on the icy hearth.

Chimneys

All that remain
are chimneys,
blackened brick statues
standing among the ashes.
Dark reminders of the need
for warmth
in winter.

How ironic
these smoke tunnels
survived
the deadly inferno.

A different winter came,
a manic frenzy,
raging, suffocating.
Nature devouring its own.

Drought Breaking

Rain came
this morning
like a blessing
purifying
everything
to clarity.
The world was
transformed,
shining, sublimely
blue.

Holiday

Just as a wave rises and falls
so does a holiday come and go
leaving its trail:
a beach bag on a canvas chair,
salty towels flapping in the wind,
empty bottles filling the bin.

Grapes plucked from the vine,
flowers withered on a grave.

Christmas Eve Monarch

A splendid monarch
bronze wings edged black and
as big as a silver eye
flew past me
to hover,
for a moment,
above the lavender.
I watched it
circle the garden,
dipping and soaring,
tantalising me.
I thought of Psyche
and felt
a dear departed soul
had flown in
to say,
'Hello!'

Dancing

Please don't compare
what I feel
to a cigarette
left to burn out.

What I feel
cannot be contained
in a manufactured tobacco tube
wrapped in paper
held between someone's fingers,
or balanced on an ashtray,
smoke drifting
until all that's left is the filter end,
a stain, a stale smell, ash.

No, what I feel
is as constant, endless
as the ocean's
ebb and flow.
So, I may be dumped
a few times,
but in the main,
I'm dancing.

A Musing

My muse
is an angel
who, from time to time,
takes me unawares.

A flash of sunlit wings
casts shadows
on an empty page.
Patterns play,
rhythms whisper,
'Angel, hello.'

Visitors

Sometimes the words,
the images
rush in
tumbling over each other
in their excitement
to form meanings.
Sometimes they arrive
when you least expect them
and you have to
make the most of the opportunity,
even though it may not
be convenient.
Sometimes they amble in
one or two at a time
with no apparent connection
yet casually arrange themselves
into an easy pattern.
Sometimes they hang back
and need coaxing.
You can feel the discomfort
yet can't leave them alone.
Sometimes no amount of cajoling
will persuade them
to enter.
Then it's better
to let them be,
if you can.

Weeding

Rampant bindi
in the lawn.
Onion grass flaunting
white blossoms
while choking
the rockery.
I pull and dig.

I want to see:
green grass, weed free;
the rockery's
sculpted structure.
It's like working
with wanton words,
pulling them out
and digging deep
to find and capture
moments of experience.

The Parcel

Like the change in the wind
it came this morning,
quite unexpected
and thrilling.
It was wrapped
in paper, striped pink,
all crackly
and labelled, *La Mar.*
Oh, the chic of it,
my dear.
Oh, the fumbling
to unwrap,
the frustration!
All that sticky tape,
didn't want to tear
anything.
Carefully, carefully,
aah, *voila!*
but no.
More wrapping,
Mon Dieu!
Cardboard, cellophane
and tissue,
but inside
I could see,
wheee!
Silk stockings,
champagne pale and shimmer soft,
for me, for me.
Joie de vivre!
My dear.

Public Monuments Paris

Yes, they are grand
the public monuments,
the way they spread themselves out
pompously, along the Seine's banks,
like stolid, complacent, civic-minded
middle-aged men after lunch
overstuffed with richness.
No wonder Eiffel dreamed that tower.

Paris

You could never say,
'Paris flaunts herself',
though when you think of
the Moulin Rouge,
hmmm, but no,
that's just an aspect of Paris.
Paris as a whole
is a more
subtle seductress,
elegantly wrapped,
like chocolates from Fauchon
as she strolls
along and away from
the banks of the Seine,
confident and controlled
with exquisite manners,
'*Bonjour, Monsieur!*'
'*Bonjour, Madame!*'
At least, at first,
that's how she strikes you.

After a while, however,
you notice,
against a cacophony of frantic traffic,
signs of stress:
the cracks in the mask,
the constant smoking,
wary looks,
pushing and shoving
always with a polite
'*Pardon, Monsieur!*'
Nevertheless,
signs of stress.
The seductress, you observe,
has flaws
and becomes human.

Paris Facades

Long windows,
to catch the light,
decorative iron safety rails
made to look like balconies,
on building after building,
rows upon rows of endless buildings,
all the same,
all the same,
so correct,
so correct.
Safety in sameness
is that what it is?
How absurd
we are to think
the external
that important.

Waves

Swimming

We came to
the edge.
We looked.
The waves were huge.
We paused,
then in we plunged.

Moon-swollen
the tide surged and
swept us away.

Where are you?
Do you swim still?
Other swimmers have
not seen you.
Did your fear drown you
as mine
almost did?

The tide
took you.
Will it
return you?
I swim still
hoping.
Who can be sure...
of anything
in this vast ocean.

Sighting

An unexpected shape,
a shadow of a difference plays
near the surface of the sea.
In the eye's far corner
attention is brought to
that spot,
that infinitesimal speck
of movement,
of something extra,
something special now present.
What is it?
A soul key,
an elusive image,
a sleek seal slipping
in and out of
the waves.
Oh, the effort
it takes,
the stillness, the struggle to
hold the sighting
until it hooks
a moment of experience.
Oh! The thrill of reeling
in the catch,
from the sea's expanse.

Song of the Sea

In me
it is the song of the sea.

The languid lap, lap, lap
the endless thump, thump, thump
beating out hot nights.

A sumptuously seductive
sweet swishing foaming sweep
of fizzing froth,
a slow, swelling surge
swirling to a whip, whip, whooping,
rip, rip, ripping roar,
breaking, plummeting
in a pounding, crushing crash.

It is the song
in me
the song,
the song of the sea.

Green

I am lost
in green:
the clear, clean green
of the sea on a grey winter's day
when the waves smash
white from a long
translucent tunnel
that calls to the seeing heart,
'I am green,
I am green.'

Shadow

What is it?
That immense shifting shadow,
a whale?
Closer it comes,
close enough almost to touch.
Parts of it break the surface,
and I see!
I see!
Masses, just masses of fish.
Layers upon layers
rising with the waves,
some leap above them
like drunken sailors dancing.
Pure, pristine,
echoes of an innocent world,
untouched, supreme.

That night came the question,
'What's for dinner?'
The answer,
'Fish.'

Warning

The water is murky.
A vicious swell is rocketing
surf far up the beach
churning
flotsam, sandcastles,
dreams.

Weak swimmers; observe only.
Others…enter with caution.

This Night

The wind is still,
a high sea roars,
a cough breaks
in a sick man's chest,
waves crash to shore.

Swimmer

Moving parallel to the shore,
a lone swimmer
like some exotic fish, languidly
rises and falls with
with the waves,
unthreatened
by the bruised and violent sky;
its blackness intensifying
the green of the sea,
the white of the surf.
Perhaps the ocean's clarity
is more potent than
an approaching storm.
Oh, to be a swimmer
in a clear, green sea.

Little Seal

I saw you this morning,
fifty metres out,
gliding under the surface
just where I swim,
summer and autumn.

I stopped.
Sure enough, up you popped
with that 'Here I am!' stance
audiences love.
I waited, you dipped,
slipped under, disappeared.
You showed again,
much closer this time,
two waves from shore.
Excited now, I expected you
to ride in
on the next wave,
but no, little furry showman,
you tricked me!
You surfaced
seventy metres out.

I dreamed of what
I didn't see,
that submerged journey
to the deep,
and wondered what
unseen force,
rising from the depths,
propels us on
a different course far
from the seeming safety
of the shore.

Little seal,
does your instinct tell you
that if our safety is within,
the most fearsome depths
can be explored?
Little seal, ah…if
you could tell us
what you know.

Occasional Wave

From a flat, dead sea
an occasional wave
rears and breaks
just as in everyday lives
rare moments of bliss
come and go.

I say,
let there be more
rearing and breaking,
coming and going
to and from
bliss.

Next Wave

Big waves,
showy lines
of cancan dancers
advance, frothing
frenzied foam.
A relentless roll,
they come
crashing, smashing, pounding
to shore.

Yet often,
almost unnoticed,
the next wave,
smaller, quieter
wets your feet.

Starry Night

Stars spiral,
the earth spins
and a massive moon,
a solid, heavy wheel
blazes white
thinning black space to blue.
Wind whirls across land,
bulging waves,
black and glittering
race to endless shore.

Show Stopper

Curved lines of
fish-scale clouds
cover the sun.
Near the Indian Ocean's shore
a troupe of six dolphins cavort,
varying their act
until the sleek star
bursts up in
a perpendicular leap
before performing a
perfect diving arc to
re-enter the flat sea
in a show-stopping splash.

This Morning Early

Where the crumpled cliff
rises from
a dark and tranquil sea,
the sun glinted
across the paddle
of a man
in a canoe
shadowing two dolphins
dipping in and out
in timeless rhythm
along the reef's edge.

How many others
have stood in this place,
saw what I saw
and felt its wonder?

Waves

There are more waves,
woman,
reach out,
don't be frightened.
Don't let that dumper
mangle you forever.

So you're jangled,
woman.
Well,
what did you expect?
If you will go
for the big ones.

Watch out,
woman!
Nearly went again.
Keep your wits about you,
can't you?
This is a big, wild sea
you're in.

Dive through the centre,
woman.
That's better.
And again, good.
Once more,
see! The water's calmer here.
Float awhile.
Now strike out,
go on.
You can do it!
And don't let another dumper
dump you.

Seasons

Intimations

The bitter, grey cold
has gone.
A clean,
green, gentle day
is here
full of leaves rustling:
doves' flutterings
and the slow swishing sea.

In the thin blue sky,
clusters of strange,
white shapes float
across the sun.

Spring Afternoon in the Garden

As I pull weeds
a bronze butterfly balances
on a lavender stem,
wattlebirds swoop and shriek,
lizards loll in the sun,
a sea breeze moves
the jasmine
spreading its scent and
the last mandarin falls.

As I pull weeds
a butcher bird dives,
clouds cover the sun.
A girl blows herself up in Israel,
sirens scream in Iraq,
children lie dying of hunger.
In Bali the stench of burnt flesh
is remembered.
But…I pull weeds.

Warm Evening in Spring

How the cars rush
up the coast
on this warm spring evening.
Slow down, I say,
take your time,
and see, really see
the ocean, made more dramatic
by the wind
and bobbing surfers,
the endless sky,
the setting sun,
the full, risen moon.

Spring is Driven From the Land

A brief blossoming it was.
Now the flowers are scattered,
crushed, ravaged,
their seeds buried.
The land is barren,
seared and blackened
by devouring fires,
her weeping wounds
gouged by the steel-studded roll
of power-maddened tanks.

Despair not.
Another Spring will come
and millions of seeds,
nourished deep in the dark earth,
will push up. Up
to a mighty blossoming.

It is only
a matter of time.

Goings and Comings

Doors closing,
the lilies are fading,
flowers spent,
leaves bent,
spring is going.

Doors opening,
the agapanthus are bursting
their skins.
See the blue
pushing through.
Summer's a coming.

In Summer

Sea-dazed eyes
trace dolphins
lingering along
reefs of dreams.
White-breasted cormorants
bob the ocean's surface.
Warm scented winds
bring echoes of other
summers, other
sea-fast spaces.
Waves wash dark memories
over the sand
to shrivel
in the sun.

Late Afternoon

It is hot,
the sky is overcast,
the sea is grey and still.
A storm is coming.
Three Chinese girls
swim and laugh.
Sleek black hair
reminds me of seals,
cool breezes.

Summer's End

Sucked by the sun,
caught by the wind
a lone tumble-weed rolls
across the sand
to the sea.
Tossed higher,
over the waves it
careers madly,
rests briefly
before resuming
its glorious dash
to oblivion.

Late Heat

It is hot.
According to the calendar
summer is over.
Does the sun know this?
Leaves are burnt,
roses wilt,
even the aphids are gone.

In the evening
a man and a woman,
thighs touching
blood rising,
long for union.
Too late, too hot.

April

Here in the south,
April is the sweetest month,
the mighty earth is still.
Birds call, leaves fall,
ripe mandarins wait to be picked.
Winter is coming.

Winter's Rule

Call up the clouds,
mask the sun,
disrupt the sea,
whip up a storm.

Let the wind roar,
rain pour,
the sea race,
winter's here.

Wild Night

Winter blasted into
my garden last night.
A demented Zeus
roared through trees,
howled round the house
raining venom,
tearing ripe mandarins
to the ground.
Prometheus, where are you?

Storm Damage

The sea is wild today.
Crashing waves trail
billowing veils of spray.
Two fishermen are missing.
Broken wreaths of kelp
ripped from the reef
decorate a burial ground.
Black clouds obliterate the sun.

In the garden
storm-tossed mandarins,
bruised, battered, smashed,
litter the wet earth.
Winter has come.

Winter

Seeps
into the bones,
drips steadily
into the heart
cold, numbing,
dull winter
amid blue skies,
foaming waves,
turquoise seas.

Winter Chill

Bare is the vine.
Blue is the sky.
Bright sun
cannot defeat
withering winds
from the east.

A Winter View

It's conventional
to equate winter
with death, misery, passivity,
but something's missing,
something's wrong.
A refusal, a failure
to see winter
as something as real and wild
as a raging sea,
a southerly blow,
birds wheeling,
rain teeming,
red berries gleaming.
Death has no particular season,
winter has a life of its own.

Spring Leaves

Reaching out,
stretching, unfurling,
transparently tender,
and young, how very young,
shiny, unspoiled, new born from
a sumptuous surge,
a warm, wild urge
that's spring.

Flora

Nasturtiums

There's no other word for it,
a nasturtium
is jaunty.

Like a woman
in a new hat
or a man,
flattered by a woman
in a new hat.
Just as jaunty
as that.

Cheeky almost
and bright
saying, 'Look at me!
I'm smart
don't you think?'

And I do think so,
I have to agree.
Their deep round green,
their red, orange and yellow,
their frilly edges
are just the sauciest things
trumpeting the spring.

Mad Myrtle

Have you no shame, woman?
Flaunting yourself
in purple and green.
Purple and green!
Have you no restraint?
You cloying harlot.
The archetypal clinging vine,
you spread yourself
everywhere.
Pushy, possessive, destructive
denizen of a steamy world.

Yet, you're pretty.
Oh yes!
What a pity.
No, there's no use pleading,
Mad Myrtle,
you'll have to go.

Mad Myrtle Replies

So, I have to go
do I?
What a pity.
I mean,
I'm so pretty
in my purple and green.
Yes, in my purple and green
I make heads turn,
especially yours.

Well, I never was
for the faint-hearted,
those who feel threatened
by my wild-green power
reaching deep.
Frightened you are.
Coward.
Well, I'm off!
Off 'to fresh woods
and pastures new'.

Mad Myrtle's End

(Apologies to Wordsworth)

Trailing clouds of poison
he came,
to finish Mad Myrtle,
or 'Morning Glory'
as many know her.

How innocent she seems
In her purple and green,
how sweet her display.
Can it really be
she who causes
such trouble, upheaval,
to bring a man
to this extreme?
Mad Myrtle,
I feel mean.

Sweet William

You are not as you seem,
Sweet William,
with your stiff stalks
and pom-poms of green prickles.
For I have touched you,
Sweet William,
and your prickles are pliant
and soft.
Then when your blossoms open
in thick red clusters,
why!
How handsome you are,
Sweet William.

Frangipani

A lover's kisses
tickle my skin,
a melon cocktail
slides over my tongue.
I suck your creamy
blossoms
until I am so full
I cannot breathe.

Lavender

I look at lavender,
rampant, exuberant, gregarious,
glorious, gorgeous purple
revelling in the sun's warmth,
bees and butterflies hovering
drunk on its perfume
and wonder about
those sepia images of
stiff Victorian women,
constricted by corsets.

Did they wish to
be abandoned to the sun, too?
Is that why
they sprinkled their linen
with lavender?
To conjure up
space and ways impossible?

Red Geranium

In this harsh climate
you can rely on
a geranium.
Neither drought nor storm
can destroy it.
Really, a geranium
is extraordinary.
Break off a piece,
put it in the ground and
you'll see
how well it grows
without pampering;
though a little pampering
never hurt anyone,
not even a geranium
which can survive years of neglect
and while this might make it
stunted and scrawny;
never mind
it's alive
and declares this
perennially
with round furry leaves
and that red;
that impudent show of scarlet.

To a Viola

In our gardens
we feel like gods.
We plant seeds,
we watch them sprout,
we pull out weeds,
crush snails and other pests,
to stop their rout.
We are in control.

But what of seeds
planted by the wind or birds
in unsuitable places?
A delicate viola,
its blueness interrupting
the perfect green lawn.
What do we do with that?
Do we wonder how it pushed up
through the dense mat of roots?
Do we appreciate its strength,
its ability to blossom
in hostile territory?
Do we remove it
because it does not fit?
Do we carefully ease it free,
transplant it to a congenial spot
where we can more comfortably
admire its colour,
its slender beauty?

Some of us,
like that viola,
blossom in foreign territory.
Some of us
like that green lawn,
are fed and cut to perfection,
complacent, until a seed sprouts
where it should not.
And some of us are not one
nor the other
but something else entirely.
Let us be thankful for that.

Leaves

The Mandarin Tree

Here you are,
envoy of old China,
in my garden by the sea.
Dignified in glossy green and
glowing orange, radiating
your badge of office and identity.
Mandarin, mandarin.

You stand
offering me fruit.
You tolerate
the hot east wind in summer,
the salt wind from the south
and sandy soil
beneath this brick-paved courtyard
enclosed with limestone.

You were born
in some antique Emperor's court,
filled with fountains, caged nightingales
and silk-clad women,
hair upswept with jewelled combs,
sipping jasmine tea from fine porcelain.
Your presence delighted them.
They praised you in sweet songs.

What brought you here?
Did you wing it
with a migrating bird
who dropped you on the way
to choicer parts?

I do not know.
But here you are,
transplanted and flourishing,
and here I am,
looking and wondering.

Fallen Mandarin

Last night
a whirling dervish
of a wind
whipped the mandarin tree,
stripped and spun
its last fruit
to the brick path
splitting its skin.

In a moment, we
too can be
ripped from innocence,
flung to a hard place
and broken open.

Banksia

Enigmatic denizen
of an ancient land,
quiet witness shaped
into fierce postures
by harsh winds.
Rough bark and jagged leaves,
lit by intricate candles
circled by butterflies,
fluttering.
Gentle warrior,
singing secrets
to the sun.

Casuarina Equisetifolia

Why is it
that you,
with your grand, mellifluous name,
should live in this desolate,
exposed place
by the sea?

Swaying with the wind,
swooning in brown melancholy,
weeping, sweeping sand endlessly,
you are as hauntingly beautiful
as the 'Ave Maria'
and as enduring.

Perhaps, only you,
could bear
to live here.

A View

Caught in a rainbow
pine trees
glow
but as different from
Christmas trees
as is the sea
from a fish pond.

The Pine

Is a favourite
of mine.
A balance of boughs
in sculpted space
surpasses the anarchy
of wattles.

I like
the pine's cleansing scent,
the stillness that comes
from its dark greenness.
Salt winds, snow,
heat, drought
are nothing to it.
Crows like it too.

Near the Mandarin Tree

On this warm spring afternoon
sun shines golden on nasturtium leaves,
lizards scurry under eaves,
birds fly in pairs.
Everywhere, there are blossoms
filling the air with perfume.
Near the mandarin tree I sit
and think of you.

Under the Mandarin Tree Again

Here I am
under the mandarin tree again
thinking of you.
Thinking how good
it would be
if we could
walk for a while
and every now and then,
sit and talk
of unimportant
and important things.
The beach would be the place,
about six in the evening
when it's still.
That's the time
to see dolphins dipping,
the sun slipping,
the world tipping.

On Watering a Mandarin Tree

Some loves promise much
but fail
to swell and sweeten.
Incompatible strains
they fall,
small, green and bitter.
So,
best to graft
to new stock.
A harvest
may yet be gathered.

Canopy

Splendid word,
generous sound,
sheltering image,
leafy branches spreading out,
green mosaics
studded with blue
casting intricate shadows
across grey walls.
A tree in our city.

Observation

Devoid of green,
grotesquely elegant,
a gaunt branch extends
an intricate fan of stiff twigs
against the endless sky,
papery leaves
shake precariously.

Little Almond Tree

Black is the night.
The sea's roar
rushes in
time after time,
filling silence and
in a dream
I see
a little almond tree
in blossom,
pale petals
flooding emptiness
with light.

Heartsick

Tree, you are sick,
your leaves,
a brittle network of veins,
fall without colour.
You are being
eaten up,
your heart sucked out
by creatures
growing fat
on your sap.
Handsome once,
hollow now,
can your deep roots
save you?
Oh, let a savage wind
blow a ravaging
seducer to bewitch
your killers
into letting go.

Olive Tree

Let's drink to this
sturdy, shapely,
generous and tough
Mediterranean symbol
of renewal.
Remember Noah and the dove?
This treasure of a tree
prefers warm places
to convert sunlight into
berries full of thick,
rich oil
beloved of cooks.
Its uses endless,
its wealth,
our health.

The Dancing Tree

In mad pagan celebration
from one thick base,
two sloping trunks
thrust heavenwards.
Sinuous brown limbs
sprouting, green Dionysian crowns,
couple wantonly.

Jacaranda

How can I find words
for the colour
of a jacaranda
in blossom?
More purple than blue
but not oppressively so
like the velvet robes
of kings and queens.
Perhaps, somewhere between
the purple of monarchs
and the summery blue
of agapanthus.
Joyous, shot through with light,
no heaviness at all.
'Gloria in Excelsis Deo'.

The Mandarin Tree is Blossoming

'Enough of blood and tears!'
The mandarin tree is blossoming.
How sweet it scents the sunlight,
how fine its green space
in the blue sky.
Young leaves
sprout madly to heaven,
what promise is
swinging in the wind.

Feathers

New Holland Honeyeater

The sea is quiet today.
Above the blue horizon
a banner of smog hangs.
Near the cliff's edge
a little honeyeater
darts among prickly wattle,
its yellow throat blending with the blossoms.
From time to time it pauses,
Alert, pert.

Not far away
streams of cars
release filthy fumes.
Do you see what I see?

Let us not be driven to destroy.
No. Let us be driven by the joy of seeing
a little black and yellow bird
drinking nectar.

Owl

In night's abyss,
I hear you call,
'Boo book, boo book,'
comforting, haunting.
Like me you are awake
but unlike me
you're ready to strike
a mouse or rat,
while I,
I wrestle with questions.
I think of your eyes
round, fathomless pools
linked to wisdom
since ancient times.

Once in the dusk
your feathers brushed
my cheek
as soft as a sigh
for a hunter with
talons made to kill.

Another time, at a similar hour,
you flew down and perched
on a canvas chair
next to me.
We sat until
full darkness engulfed us.
In silence you took flight,
a breath escaped my lips.

You, I see, are certain
of your purpose.
I consider and am moved to ask,
'Symbol of Athena,
what are humans for?'

Dove

I sing not
of Picasso's symbol,
but of the little wood dove
plumply brown and grey,
the one who calls gently
to her mate
and to others who may hear.
Comforting and companionable,
she whirrs her way
to nest and feed,
unobtrusive, quiet,
a little brown love.

Caspian Terns

Rare visitors to
the Sorrento shore
four of them, red-legged,
stand at the water's edge
preening their grey and white feathers
with long red beaks.
Every now and then
the four take off
for a spin
in a wide arc
over the ocean and
return to land
at the same spot.
How gratifying
to be
in the right place
at the right time.
We can miss so much
without even knowing.

Twenty Eights: Ring-necked Parrots

Absolutely fabulous
they are,
in glowing emerald
with touches of yellow and red,
perfectly placed
for contrast,
and a wicked black cap
to show off the bright eyes.

You can't help but
admire their piercing whistles.
They demand attention
as they swoop
in their indiscriminate attacks,
scattering leftovers
triumphantly
in their crazy wake
like mad housewives,
creating chaos
out of order.

Flamingo

If I were a rooster
I'd ooze envy
for the flamingo's
fluid flamboyance and
leggy style,
the perfect pinkness of it:
the razzle, dazzle
of the flock
massing thick
by languid lakes,
long, curving formations
of pink clouds
rising, challenging the gods.
Yes, if I were a rooster
I'd give up crowing
for good.

Roosters

Have you noticed
how they strut,
and stretch their necks
before they crow,
looking beadily
from each side
for their audience?

Have you noticed
the sleek, glossy
cock's plumage,
the black tail feathers
well preened,
in place,
ready for the display?

Have you noticed
the spurs
ready to strike,
The red flashy comb,
red fleshy wattles
dangling slack, flapping
like diseased testicles?

Have you noticed
how they set
each other off?
Crow upon crow
trying to be top toff,
never knowing when to stop?
Showing off, puffed up
like pompous, cocky men.

Galah

In Scotland, a gala,
with emphasis on the 'ga',
is a festival,
a place, a time
for celebration.

In Australia, a galah,
is an affectionate insult
for stupidity in a person.
It is also the common name for
a particular cockatoo,
pink and grey
and comical to us.
It can even say,
'Hello, Cocky!'
if taught and other
less acceptable things.

I like to think that late one night,
a migrant Scot
in her cups
was so filled with delight
by the cockatoo's rocking dance
that she said,
with emphasis on the 'la',
'Come on you great gala
show us what you can do!'
Merging celebration and bird
forever,
'For auld lang syne.'

Magpie

What a singer it is
warbling its welcome to the day
with full throated panache,
calling up other mornings,
other places.
A seducer spinning a spell
who swoops
to wound its victims,
the Machiavelli of the bird world,
a black and white bandit
who would have your eyes.
View magpies
through glasses.

Canary

Do you remember
where you come from,
canary in a cage
singing so sweetly?

Do you remember,
yellow prima donna of the bird world,
flying free in mild,
exotic islands?

Do you remember,
little gleam of sunshine,
perching high in slender trees,
the rising moon, the setting sun?

Do you remember,
the smell of the sea
the feel of the wind
the sound of the rain?

Oh! Little yellow songbird,
is all you remember
the faces peering at you
through the bars of your cage?

Oh canary! Sweet canary,
does it matter
if you cannot remember
what you have lost?

Cormorant

From a window
a woman,
knife in hand,
watches a cormorant
near the water's edge
fan its feathers
seductively, across the sand.

Dreamily she cuts open
a plump, purple passionfruit
for the sweet seedy flesh.
'Tart!' she declares.
The bird takes off.

Penguins

Don't they look trim
in their black tuxedos
standing on rocks
at the edge of the sea
rolling with the wind?
How splendid a din,
a colony of musicians
drunk on gin,
tuning up,
wings like sleek fins
moving to the beat
of some distant drummer;
preparing for the swimphony,
the silent music of the deep.

Silver Eyes

I've been waiting
for them and
they've been waiting
too, for the black grapes
to ripen.
Today, they arrived.
A sortie of
little brown marauders,
darting into the vine,
eyes rimmed in silver,
needle-sharp beaks
piercing the purple skins
for the juice.
I clapped
and off they flew.
I'll be ready again,
tomorrow.

Red-capped Plover

Under a sullen sky,
on a sombre summer sea
stretched flat
to the horizon
where container ships lie,
two canoeists glide south
paddles dipping
in and out.

At the sea's edge,
I smile.
A tiny bird,
its pin-thin legs pumping,
darts back and forth
rosy head bent,
pecking at morsels
invisible to me.
Even now, weeks later
I smile.

Two Little Birds

One morning,
outside my window
on the bare grapevine
two willie-wagtails
build a silvery nest.
I imagine the eggs,
fledgelings and flying lessons
to come.
I am blest.

On the third day,
a thieving magpie,
eyes darting, head twitching,
lands on the vine,
It does not sing.
The willies bombard it.
It does not move.

To the rescue I rush,
too late, too late.
The magpie swoops,
tears a tuft from
the silky nest and flies off
flouting the wagtails'
zapping pursuit.

The willies return
in the morning.
For three more days,
piece by piece,
they dismantle their work,
flying it to a new site.

On the bare grapevine
a few silvery threads remain.

After Last Night's Storm

In my garden
it is still.
Ripe mandarins lie
scattered, cracked open
on the wet earth.
A red wattlebird
uses its curved bill
to suck their juice.
On the brick path
a willy-wagtail jigs,
fans its tail.
Two laughing doves
whirr to the
peppermint tree.
These birds know
nothing of the plague
sweeping the world.
For a moment
neither do I.

Sentients

Wedding Dance

Beautiful were
the bridesmaids' breasts
but it was
their arms
that transfixed me.

Slender and supple,
swans' necks swaying,
flawless, innocent,
yet with the power
to bring a man
undone.

Sounds

Breaking the sounds
of wind and waves,
a woman escaping chaos,
plays Schubert to
boys beating tin drums
as loose timbers bang
on a house
by the sea.

Dune Woman

Behind the dunes
she sits,
the woman with wild brown hair,
no wind can catch her there.
She reads.
She does not
respond to greetings.
A ragged daisy,
seen but unseeing,
her sun-stained face
speaks pain,
too sore
to share.

Blues

Lift your head,
woman, come,
look up, see the shimmering ocean's
exquisite blues,
heart piercing
mind freeing
unbearably blue
woman, come,
lift your head,
look up.

Grown Up

Because I am grown up
I have not spoken
of the pain,
I have hidden
it within.
A child again,
weeping only
in the silence
of my room.

But…I am grown up
and will not
burden you.

Butterfly

Come, you cannot be imprisoned
in that dark cocoon.
Your colours, your glory
are meant
to be seen.

Trust the urge to spread
your wings.
It will guide you
to the light,
the space
and air you need to flutter,
float in.

Come, do not
tremble.
Leave behind
that black hole.
Come,
launch yourself.

Fireworks

He looked at her.
The spark ignited a rocket.
A multicoloured trail
lit an arc of stars.

She looked at him,
no spark,
no light in the dark.
A damp squib,
no fizz.

Call To Prayer

At sunrise
in a foreign country
a man swimming slowly
lap after lap
in a blue pool
calls up
in my home country
a lone fisherman
casting into
a blue ocean
time after time.

Ties

I don't mind being
tied to you.
Most of the time
it feels good,
perfect, even
when you accidentally
spill something on me,
I don't feel soiled,
stains like that
lift off easily,
but when
you remove me
and put me away carelessly
in a dark drawer or closet
because I don't suit you,
or your suit,
I am fit to be tied
and want to
break out and shout,
'Get knotted!'

So in the darkness
unseen, unheard,
I seethe and scheme
how I will teach you not
to discard me thoughtlessly.

When next you pluck me out
to decorate your neck
I will choke you.
I see the headline,
'Garrotted by own tie'
how neat,
how sweet.

Today William

(for Wordsworth)

My heart leaped up.
I heard thee
in the call of the sea.
And William
on the roar of the wild wind
I called thee,
in full, skying flight,
battered and lashed,
I sang, I sang
in the wild wind,
for the raging sea
and thee.
And thee.

On Sorrento Beach

One summer's day
a burly, black-haired man strode over the sand.
A colossus, he found a spot,
dropped to his knees,
put down his towel
on top of his newspaper and
began building
a sandcastle.
There were no children,
it was just for himself.
A broad, symmetrical shape grew.
When the structure was finished
he draped it with his towel,
sat down, leaned backed against it, adjusted himself,
picked up and read his newspaper.

Little Boat

(for my father)

Mad, battering rain
attacks the little sail boat.
How sturdy she is.

Savage winds whip her,
cruel waves curl over her.
How gallant she is.

Heading for harbour,
a grey bird circles above.
Alone she sails on.

Under the Warm Earth

He lies silent
in a wooden box.
Eyes unseeing,
limbs stiff, cold.

Blue or starry skies,
waves crashing,
a sea breeze on his skin, and
jasmine-laden air
are not for him.

He lies
full of stories
he can tell no more.
In summer he was buried.
A stone marks his grave.

Cast My Ashes

On the water
where the waves
break and tumble
to the beach.

Choose a blue day,
a gentle day,
glistening,
an April day
like this.

Cast my ashes
so that
the waves play
with them
a little.

Watch them
wash to shore
at this place
I have loved
so much.

Song of Eden

A biblical garden,
trees, forbidden fruit,
a man, a woman
beguiled by a subtle serpent.
Paradise lost.

A corner café,
stuffed wings of chicken,
seafood steamboat,
coriander, Chinese tea.
Paradise regained.

This Man

He shows me wonders
unspoken,
this man
in a wheelchair:
doves feeding,
a red geranium,
clothes flapping on the line,
clouds and the blue sky.
This broken man is
unbroken.

For Kate

Well, dear heart,
your latest paintings
made me think.
They told me a story
of lost romance, lost magic.

For me the story begins
in Venice,
or maybe that's where it ends?
That would be more hopeful
and you did place that painting
near the end of the series.
Old, colourful stately Venice:
gondola, canal, palaces, bridges
softly shimmering
blue, gold and rich, red ochre.
Yes, touches of rich, red ochre
I seem to remember,
though the memory
does play tricks.
Anyway, as I was saying,
Venice, a marvellous backdrop
to romance, possibilities.
Some sixteen paintings or so
and only two in colour!
The one of Venice,
and even that a reproduction.

154

What is going on here?
and the other seemingly
less representational, more impressionistic,
golden, blue, glowing,
placed next to it.
What a contrast to the rest:
the black and white images,
the formal couples waltzing;
the chandeliers and the empty goblets,
were they Venetian too?
Haunting, ghostly
imitations of images,
is there no end to imitation?
Is there no reality but this?
Memories of magic,
shallow shadows,
dreams, leeched of colour?

No, dear heart,
this I do not believe.
I believe,
most strongly,
the magic is not lost.
It is real.
It is there in you.
How else
could you paint
the way you do?

The Bath

Five p.m., Friday,
he unlocks the door,
walks into silence.
No one is home.
He sighs with relief,
takes off his coat,
draws the curtains,
puts a match to the fire,
watches weak flames
sneak up the twigs,
selects a CD. Soon
Götterdämmerung beats on his brain.
He pours a scotch,
goes to the bathroom,
turns on the taps,
comes back to the lounge,
lies on the couch
and waits
for his Rhine to fill up.

Laden with shopping,
and a baby, whining,
she opens the front door,
'Hi, Darl! I'm home.'
Soaped up, lying back,
eyes shut, soaking,
he calls through the steam,
'I'm in the bath!'

In the kitchen,
she lights the cooker,
unpacks shopping
item by item,
stows it away,
feeds the child,
puts him to bed,
makes a phone call,
chops chicken,
slices carrots and onions,
arranges in casserole,
adds stock and seasoning,
puts dish in oven,
sets the table, calmly.

Wrapped in a towel,
he saunters in.
'Anything wrong, pet?'
'No, dear. Your dinner's in the oven.
I've rung Fleur.
I'm meeting her
at Jim's Bar.
I've just got
to get out of here!'

Urban Cowboy

I saw him
swagger over
out of the slow lane,
with his trusty steed;
black, with a
spunky rear end,
its high slung
classy chassis
icon of an optimistic time,
solid, generous,
shiny and showy,
saddled for fun.

Rower

Lurching against the tide
a lone rower
heads out.
Grey, numbing cold
blasts out salt air
from the west.
Spray shrouds him.
What quest
drives him on?

Things People Say

I heard someone say,
'Did you know
butterflies need nectar?
Roses don't have nectar.
If you want butterflies
plant more than roses.'

I heard someone say,
'In Australia the sun
has different properties.
Here the sun stings the skin.
There is no sting
in the Northern sun.'
The things people say.

I say,
no sun, no roses,
no butterflies, no sting,
no thing.
I say, I say, I say.

Previously Published Poems

Spaces

'Day Breaks', *The Mozzie*, December 2015
'Sleepless', *The Mozzie*, August 2018
'Day is Beginning', *The Mozzie*, March 2015
'Awakening', *Poetry d'Amour*, WA Poets Inc, 2018
'This is just to tell you…', *Poetry on the Big Screen*, WA Poets Inc, 2019
'Path', *The Mozzie*, December 2019
'Rationality', *Westerly*, Summer 1992
'Sorrow', *Creatrix Online 52*, March 2021
'A Cold Wind', *The Mozzie*, April/May 2017
'Chimneys', *Messages from the Embers*, Black Quill Press, 2020
'Drought Breaking', *The Mozzie*, February 2021
'Holiday', *The Mozzie*, September 2017
'A Musing', *Creatrix Online 40*, 2018
'Weeding', *The Mozzie*, February 2021
'Public Monuments Paris', *The Mozzie*, April 2015

Waves

'Swimming', *Poetry d'Amour*, WA Poets Inc, 2017
'Sighting', *SWWWA Newsletter*, Bronze Quill competition, Highly Commended, 1996
'Song of the Sea', *The Mozzie*, 2017
'Green', *The Mozzie*, July 2016
'Shadow', *The Mozzie*, April 2018
'Warning', *Poetry on the Big Screen*, WA Poets Inc, 2019
'This Night', *The Mozzie*, June 2018
'Little Seal', *Earthworks and Artlinks,* online anthology, 2020

'Next Wave', *The Mozzie*, September 2020
'Starry Night', *The Mozzie*, August 2019
'Show Stopper', *The Mozzie*, January 2021

Seasons

'Intimations', *The Mozzie*, September 2014
'Spring Afternoon in the Garden', *Creatrix Anthology
    2012–2016*, WA Poets Inc, 2017
'Warm Evening in Spring', *The Mozzie*, December 2015
'Near the Mandarin Tree', *Australian Love Poetry*, Inkerman
    and Blunt, 2014
'Spring Is Driven From the Land', *The Mozzie*, October 2019
'Goings and Comings', *The Mozzie*, January/February 2019
'In Summer', *The Mozzie*, December 2017
'Late Afternoon', *The Mozzie*, December 2015
'Summer's End' and 'Late Heat', *The Mozzie*, March/April
    2016
'Wild Night', *The Mozzie*, July 2018
'Winter', *The Mozzie*, August 2017, Highly commended
    short poem in *The Mozzie* Awards 2017
'Winter Still', *The Mozzie*, April 2014
'A Winter View', *The Mozzie*, July 2017
'Spring Leaves', *The Mozzie*, October 2014

Flora

'Nasturtiums', *Fremantle Arts Review*, August 1988
'Mad Myrtle', *The Mozzie*, April 2013 and November 2013
'Sweet William', *tamba,* June 2013
'Lavender', *The Mozzie*, November/December 2019

Leaves

'Fallen Mandarin', *Creatrix Online 50*, September 2020

'Banksia', *tamba 55*, September 2014

'Casuarina Equisetifolia', *The Mozzie*, November 2016

'A View', *The Mozzie*, October 2016

'The Pine', *The Valley Micropress*, New Zealand, June 2014

'Under the Mandarin Tree Again', *The Mozzie*, July 2014

'On Watering a Mandarin Tree', *The Mozzie*, June 2014

'Canopy', *The Mozzie*, January/February 2018

'Observation', *Poetry on the Big Screen*, WA Poets Inc, 2019

'Olive Tree', *The Mozzie*, July 2017

'Jacaranda', *The Mozzie*, September/October 2019

Feathers

'New Holland Honeyeater', *The Mozzie*, April/May 2017

'Caspian Terns', *The Mozzie*, February 2021

'Flamingo', *The Mozzie*, June 2017

'Galah', *The Mozzie*, April 2019

'Magpie', *The Mozzie*, October 2018

'Cormorant', *The Mozzie*, August 2019

'Penguins', *The Mozzie,* November 2017

'After Last Night's Storm', *Creatrix Online*, May 2020

Sentients

'Wedding Dance' and 'Dune Woman', *The Mozzie*, July 2016

'Blues', *The Mozzie*, September 2013

'Grown Up', *The Mozzie*, February 2016

'Butterfly', *The Mozzie*, December 2016

'Fireworks', *The Mozzie*, January/February 2018

'On Sorrento Beach', *Digital Display*, WA Poets Inc, 2020

'Little Boat', *The Mozzie*, August 2019

'Cast My Ashes', *The Yellow Moon*, Summer 2006, Highly

commended in Spirit of Place competition
'This Man', *The Mozzie*, June 2018
'Rower', *The Mozzie*, August 2020

CPSIA information can be obtained
at www.ICGtesting.com
Printed in the USA
LVHW080752290822
726956LV00014B/395